The Roman Laws

Grandfather of Present-Day Basic Laws

Government for Kids
Children's Government Books

BABY PROFESSOR
EDUCATION KIDS

Speedy Publishing LLC

40 E. Main St. #1156

Newark, DE 19711

www.speedypublishing.com

Copyright 2017

Many of our basic ideas and systems came from Ancient Rome and several aspects of Roman Law and the Roman Constitution are around today, including regular elections, term limits, separation of powers, vetoes, and checks and balances. These concepts serve as foundations for today's democratic governments. Ancient Rome's legacy is still seen today in our western cultures, in such areas as religion, engineering, architecture, language, law, and government.

Plebeian Council

WHO MADE THE LAWS?

There were many different ways that the laws were created. Primarily, official new laws were made through Roman Assemblies. Citizens that were members of assemblies would vote on these laws. However, there were different ways, that laws could be implemented which included the Plebeian Council, decisions by elected officials, decrees by the senate, and edicts by the emperor.

WHO ENFORCED THESE LAWS?

A praetor was the official that enforced the laws. This person was the second highest official in the Roman republic, behind the consuls. He was accountable for administration of justice.

Praetor

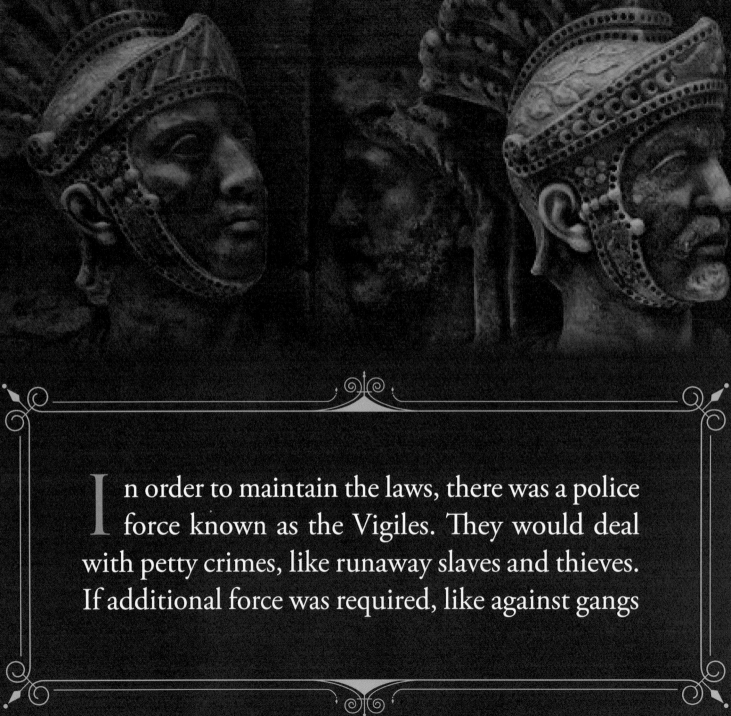

In order to maintain the laws, there was a police force known as the Vigiles. They would deal with petty crimes, like runaway slaves and thieves. If additional force was required, like against gangs

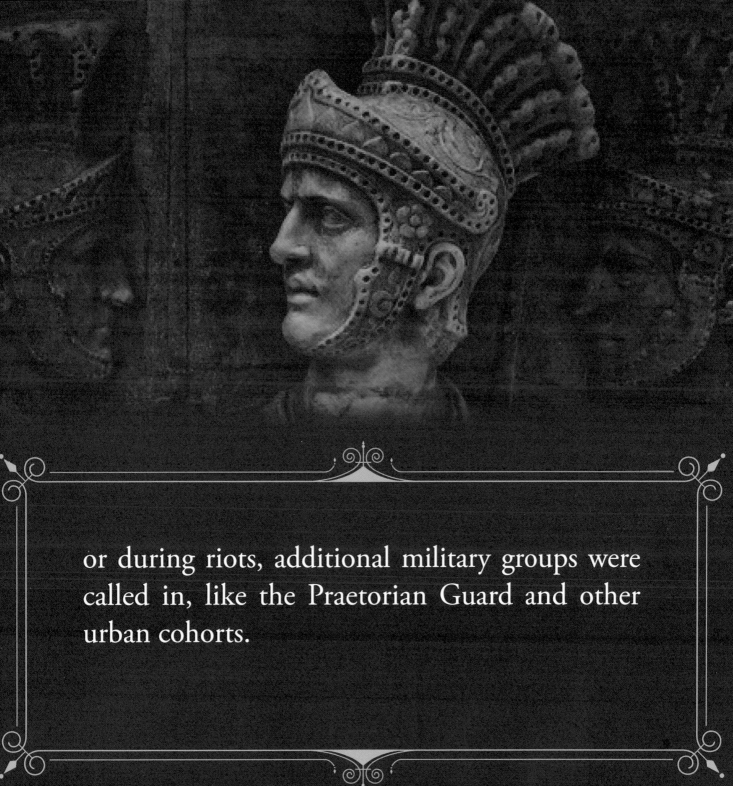

or during riots, additional military groups were called in, like the Praetorian Guard and other urban cohorts.

ROMAN CONSTITUTION

This Constitution was a set of principles agreed upon and followed by the Roman government. It had not been written down, but had been established by individual laws and tradition.

The Law of the Twelve Tables

Since many of these laws were not written down or not available to people to view, there was a lot of room for corruption by the public officials. Eventually, the people revolted and, in 450 BC, some of the laws were then written on stone tablets for anyone to read. These became known as the Law of the Twelve Tables.

Roman Citizens

Many of the rights and protections provided to people under this Roman law applied only to the citizens of Rome. To become a full Roman citizen, it was a major deal. There were different levels to the Roman citizenship, with each one having more rights than the next level.

PRISONS AND PUNISHMENT

The punishment was not the same for everyone that committed a crime in Rome. The punishment was dependent upon your status. If you were wealthy, you might receive less punishment than a slave would receive for the exact same crime.

Mamertine Prison

Punishment ranged from lashings, beatings, fines, exile from Rome, and even death. Generally, the Romans would not send a person to prison for their crimes, however, there were jails which were used to hold people while determination of the punishment or guilt was determined.

The Roman government consisted of three branches, the legislative assemblies, which was the branch of the people; the senate, which was the branch of the patricians and nobles; and the consuls, known as the executive branch.

The Roman Emperor Caracalla, in 212 A.D. declared all freedmen were now full citizens of Rome. The laws known as the Justinian Code were written down and organized and used throughout all of the empire.

Temple of Bacchus

THE ROMAN REPUBLIC

The Roman Republic governed Ancient Rome for 500 years. This type of government allowed people to elect its officials. It became complex, consisting of detailed laws, a constitution, and elected official like senators. Many of these structures and ideas have become the basis for our modern democracies.

WHO WERE ITS LEADERS?

The Roman Republic consisted of several leaders and groups helping to govern. Magistrates were elected officials and there were various titles and levels for them. This government became very complicated with many councils and leaders.

Consuls – Consuls were at the top of the Roman Republic and considered a quite powerful position. There would always be two consuls elected to prevent one from becoming a dictator or king, and they would only serve for one year. If they did not agree, they had the power to veto each other. They had many different powers, including deciding when to go to battle, how much to collect in taxes, and creating the laws.

Senators – This was a group of prestigious leaders advising the consuls. The consuls would generally do what the Senate suggested. Senators were chosen for life.

Plebeian Council - This Council was also known as the Peoples Assembly. This would be how the plebeians, the common people, could elect their leaders, magistrates, pass laws, and hold court.

Tribunes - Tribunes were delegates for the Plebeian Council. They had power to veto laws created by the Senate.

Roman Governor Domitius Corbulo

Governors – Once Rome began to conquer new lands, they would need someone to stand in as their local ruler. A governor would be appointed by the Senate to rule the province or land. This governor would then be held responsible for the local Roman army as well as being responsible for collection of taxes. They were also referred to as proconsuls.

Aedile – The city official that was in charge of maintenance for public festivals and public building was known as the Aedile. If a politician wanted to run for a higher office, he would first become an aedile so as to hold large festivals and become popular with the citizens.

Censor – The person keeping track of the number of citizens was known as the Censor. Some of their other responsibilities would include looking after public finances and maintaining public morality.

The Constitution

They did not have a written precise constitution. It worked more as a set of principles and guidelines that had passed from generation to generation. It provided for balance of power and separate branches of government.

WERE ALL PEOPLE TREATED EQUALLY?

Depending on their wealth, citizenship, and gender people were treated differently. Women had no right to hold office or to vote. The more money you had, the more voting power you would have. The Consuls, Senators, and Governors would only come from a rich aristocracy.

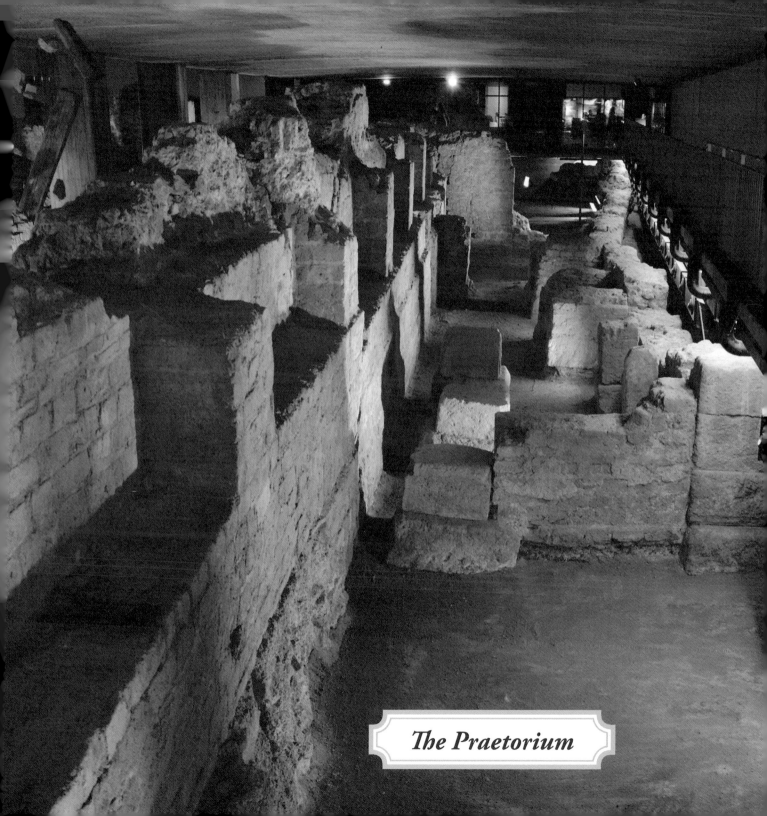

The Praetorium

While this may sound unfair, it had become a great change from the other civilizations where an average person would have no say at all. In Rome, regular citizens could join together and increase their power through their Tribunes and the Assembly.

THE ROMAN REPUBLIC GOVERNMENT

Many of today's government are modeled from the Roman Republic. Representation, veto, and balance of powers were all created and documented by the Romans.

The United States Capitol

The United States consists of three branches of government, which is comparable to the Roman Republic. The President, also known as the Executive Branch, is elected like the consuls of Rome. Congress, also known as the Legislative Branch, is elected like the Roman assemblies. The Judicial Branch is like the Praetors. The U.S. Senate is named after the Senate of Rome.

LAW

Current laws of many countries were influenced by Roman law. Civil rights, trial by jury, personal property, contracts, corporations, and legal wills were all influenced by Roman law.

LANGUAGE

At the time of the Roman Empire, Latin was spoken by the Romans and then spread throughout Western Europe. Latin terms are commonly still used in law, science, and medicine.

L atin influenced many languages and these are referred to "Romance languages". These include Romanian, Italian, Portuguese, Spanish, and French. Approximately 800 million people all over the world currently speak a Romance language.

We will use Roman numerals today. For example, the numbers used to define the number of the NFL Super Bowl is written using Roman numerals, with an exception of Super Bowl 50.

Roman numeral Analog Clock

Roman Theatre

ARCHITECTURE

Ancient Rome's architecture and buildings still have an influence over many of today's building designs. The neoclassical architecture movement during the 18th century returned to many of their ideas. The United States Capitol Building, as well as some other famous buildings, large banks, and government buildings are influenced by Roman Architecture.

Construction and Engineering

B y spreading their engineering innovations throughout the empire, they were able to change the western world. They increased trade and helped armies to move quickly around the empire by building roads that lasted. Some of these roads are used today.

Library of Celcus

Roman Aqueduct

They were also known for public projects such as building public buildings, such as bath houses. They perfected concrete so that they could build a lot of these buildings at a cheaper price than stone.

CHRISTIANITY

During the late era of the Roma Empire, there had been a big impact on the religion through spread of Christianity. Since Rome was home to the Catholic Church, it would influence Europe for the next thousand years. Christianity is currently the largest religion in the world.

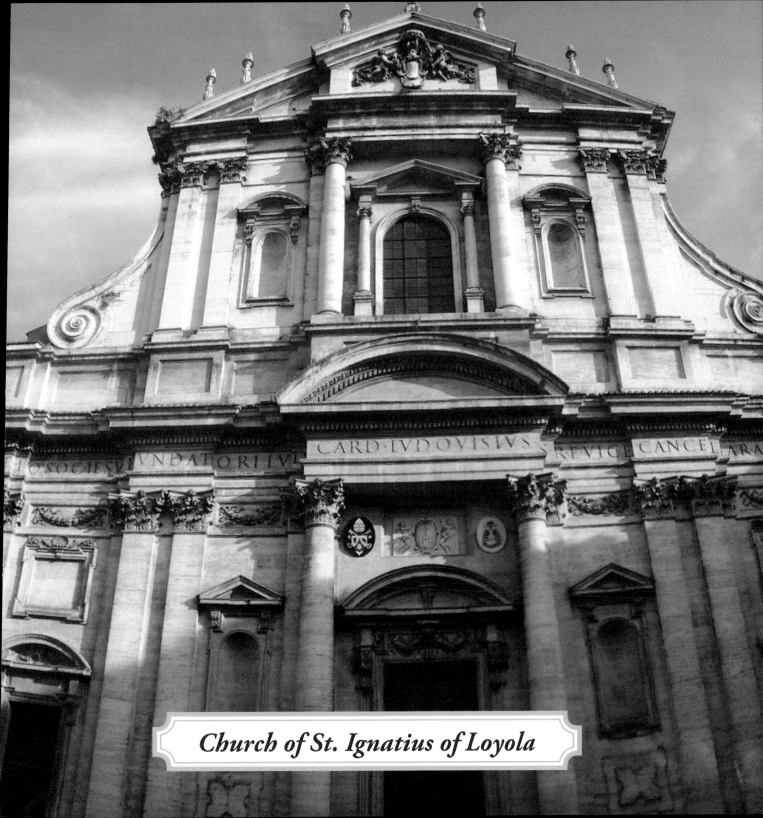

Church of St. Ignatius of Loyola

Colosseum

Rome is now the capital of Italy. It is located in the same place that was originally known as the city of Ancient Rome. If you are lucky enough to visit Rome, you will see many original buildings, including the Roman Forum and the Colosseum.

If you would like more information about this subject, you might want to research the internet, go to your local library, or ask questions of your teachers, family, and friends.

Visit

BABY PROFESSOR
EDUCATION KIDS

www.BabyProfessorBooks.com

to download Free Baby Professor eBooks and view
our catalog of new and exciting Children's Books

Printed in Poland
by Amazon Fulfillment
Poland Sp. z o.o., Wrocław